The Neuroscience of Access Consciousness®

A bridge between science and energy.

By Juanjo Suárez

AC PUBLISHING

The Neuroscience of Access Consciousness®:
A Bridge Between Science and Energy

ISBN (paperback): 978-1-63493-763-4
ISBN (eBook): 978-1-63493-764-1

Published by Access Consciousness® Publishing
www.acpublishing.com

Juan José Suarez Vinueza
@yosoy_eljuanjo

Cuenca-Ecuador
www.juanjosuarez.life

Edition: Gaby Tello
Design: MCMTech
English translation: Gabriela Marín
Prologue: Dr. Dain Heer

To each and every one of the choices that have brought me here.

To the wonderful choice of incarnating in my family. Mom, sis, you watched me change and were always supporting and smiling beside me.

To Gaby, my partner, with whom I choose to walk with day by day. To you, the one who is and lets me be. Thank you for always being that space of love and camaraderie.

To Vale, for you that knows what it is to be an infinite being, you have taught me to go all in, to only ask and be willing to receive no matter what happens around me.

To Bruno, thank you for pushing me to write this, thank you because you saw something in me that I hadn't seen.

And to this book, that with its energy and consciousness was written and given form between dreams and sleepless nights, amid science and energy.

And to you, thank you for choosing this book, for reading and sharing it.

Table of Contents

Prologue

I am truly delighted and honored to write the prologue for a book that so brilliantly bridges the worlds of science and consciousness, especially when penned by a colleague as insightful as Juanjo.

I met Juanjo in a tropical haven at El Lugar, our eco-resort in Costa Rica, where I was facilitating a six-day-long intensive event. During such events, I am usually very protective of my free time, knowing that I need space to recharge for the next day. But when Juanjo offered me a session, my body said, "Yes, please, let's try this!"

His osteopathic session was beautiful – a deeply insightful interaction with my body, delivered with a sensitivity and precision that spoke volumes. I left feeling lighter, with an even greater appreciation for the body's innate intelligence. It was clear Juanjo possessed a rare gift: the ability to perceive beyond the obvious and truly listen to what the body communicates.

This shared understanding of the body's wisdom, combined with our mutual commitment to empowering individuals, formed an immediate bond. When Juanjo unveiled his project – this book – I was instantly captivated.

I know the transformative power of Access Consciousness® tools; they work like magic. But I've also known that there is a place for a more scientific explanation for how these pragmatic tools create such rapid and profound changes. This is precisely what Juanjo has embarked upon, and he does so with exceptional clarity and elegance.

"The Neuroscience of Access Consciousness" isn't merely a theoretical exploration; it's a practical guide that illuminates how the tools of Access Consciousness interact with the very architecture of our brains and bodies. Juanjo doesn't just present the tools; he dissects the neurological mechanisms at play, making the "why" behind the "how" wonderfully comprehensible. This is invaluable for anyone curious about the astonishing potential of the human mind.

Juanjo masterfully illustrates how our ingrained responses, often born from past shocks and repetitions, shape our neural pathways and, consequently, our reality. He delves into brain waves—from the high-frequency Beta state of external focus to the slower states associated with deeper consciousness—providing a scientific framework for understanding how shifting our state of being literally changes our brain's electrical activity.

What makes Juanjo's approach truly brilliant is his ability to directly link Access tools to these neuroscientific concepts.

For example, he explains how mirror neurons lead us to unconsciously adopt others' emotions and beliefs, and how the simple question "Who does this belong to?®" acts as a neurological circuit breaker.

He demonstrates how the Ascending Reticular Activating System (ARAS) governs our attention, and how asking "What else is possible?®" and "How does it get better than this?®" redirects our ARAS, transforming it from a problem observer into a "possibility magnet."

Juanjo also explores how the Access tool "Everything is the opposite of what it appears to be, and nothing is the opposite of what it appears to be" works to deactivate the emotional charge attached to conclusions formed by the amygdala, the brain's alarm system.

Beyond the brain, Juanjo extends his scientific lens to the body itself, drawing on epigenetics and the profound role of fascia. He reveals how Access Bars® sessions, through gentle touch, influence the body's viscoelasticity, nervous system, and even its cellular memory, facilitating deep relaxation and the release of emotional trauma without cognitive re-traumatization.

This book is a testament to the fact that we are designed for transformation! It's an invitation to stop functioning from an outdated survival operating system and instead embrace a life of ease, joy, and glory.

I encourage you to step into these pages with an open mind, a curious spirit, and a willingness to question everything you thought you knew about your brain, your body, and your reality. *What if everything is way more interwoven than we've ever dared to imagine?*

With gratitude,
Dr. Dain Heer

Co-creator of Access Consciousness and developer of the energetic transformation modality *Energetic Synthesis of Being*®.

Introduction

It was December 2022, moment in which this adventure began. During those months, I found myself in a very complicated financial situation, with a blocked banking account, 3 unpaid loans and no cash in my pocket. Although my income had always been good, for some reason that I didn't understand, I couldn't have money or even make ends meet.

That moment of economic constraint didn't rob me of the motivation to record my podcast "Quebrando Cascarones"[1], in which I share with people tools I've learned throughout my life that had done me some good. For one of those interviews, I asked Bruno Reyes, an Access Consciousness Certified Facilitator, to share these tools with me, that even though I had seen Bruno work with them before, I hadn't experienced them until that moment.

After the interview, I was left very intrigued and curious about what he shared with me. One question was enough for me to ask him for a session. ***"If you could fix your life by thinking, wouldn't you have already done it?".***

We arranged a date, I stopped by an ATM and asked for a cash advance on my credit card to be able to pay for the session. « I didn't know it at the time, but my choice was to change that situation, and I was willing to do whatever it took. » Part of me kept saying, "Not again," and another part was saying, "This is the door to change, let's go for it." Obviously, I chose the latter.

During the session, Bruno introduced me to two Access Consciousness tools: "The Access Consciousness Clearing Statement" and "Light or Heavy", tools that were unfamiliar to me. At one point, my head went "Plop," and I just felt like something in my brain was

---

[1] Translator's note: this translates as "Breaking Eggshells".

short-circuiting, and I felt a kind of dizziness, while something inside me disconnected.

Today I'm writing these pages because since that session in 2022, I've been delighted with the results. My financial reality is changing, and always for the better and not only has it changed my relationship with money, but my relationships with my body, with people, with my work have also transformed. My entire life has changed.

If you're reading this, I have two possibilities:

1. You already know the Access Consciousness tools, and this book called to you.
2. You don't know them yet, and this book will help you understand the tools and how they work in your brain.

For those new to this: Access Consciousness is a set of pragmatic tools (that are used) that have a very dynamic impact on people's lives. Unlike other personal development or spiritual practices whose teachings are dogmatic (that are believed), these tools don't require of any belief; they work by simply using them, and that's what makes them more interesting.

And why do they work even if you don't believe in them? Because they are designed to transform energies and to also modulate areas of your brain, so that you awaken the full potential with which you already come pre-designed.

If you're new to the world of Access (as I'll abbreviate Access Consciousness from now on), this book will serve you as a guide to get to know some of its tools. If you're already familiar with the tools, this book invites you to recognize the potential your brain has and the change you're creating in it every time you use them.

Access is characterized by many questions and few answers. The Neuroscience of Access Consciousness is just another brand of questioning, a different possibility. It's not in itself, an answer, but it looks like one. In fact, it could be one for those who want to understand it all «group in which I include myself», for those who wonder, "What the hell is going on and why do I feel so weird when using these tools?"

And I'm telling you this because it happened to me too. I started to feel wrong, misunderstood, and even abnormal « which we have to admit, we are it », for changing so much in such short periods of time.

If you're one of those who want to understand everything, these pages will engender in you a similar chemistry to what your brain produces when you fall in love; in other words, you're going to fall in love with yourself.

If you're a seeker of new experiences and new knowledge, you might find this very interesting: the merger between the physical, chemical, and energetic.

If you're a facilitator, I invite you to use this information in your classes. It's beautiful to see people's faces when they discover that a tool enhances an area of their brain.

And if you're simply reading out of curiosity, I'll do my best to make it an entertaining read for you.

Beautiful Human Being. Welcome.

1
A Little history.
1.1 How it all started.

Changing the point of view.

"Your point of view creates your reality".
Gary M. Douglas.

Before going to your brain and the neuroscience, let me tell you what I've experienced and lay some footing.

The human body is a multisensory organism, meaning it receives thousands of bits of information per second from countless sources.

There are several communication channels, all of which have a primary function: capturing external stimuli and transforming them into electrical information. How? Through perception.

Here lies one of Access's premises. **Your point of view creates your reality.**

What we think, the mental images we have, and our internal chatter are all interpreted by our brain. Everything, absolutely everything that exists beyond our body—in the form of images, sounds, shapes, colors, smells, etc.—is interpreted by our brain and submits as a discharge of electrical current that activates neural pathways to produce hormones and neurotransmitters that respond to these stimuli.

This mechanism produces changes in both the biological (structures) and physiological (functions) aspects. When these stimuli are sustained over time and hormones are produced in larger quantities and for a prolonged period in our body, a phase of imbalance begins, which is known as "disease."

Based on this, our body does not get sick, it does not deteriorate, it is simply continuously answering to what we make real in the space between our ears.

Before Access, I had tried other modalities and taken a lot of sessions, but somehow, I would return to the familiar pattern and feel stuck again. Then I would find another practice and start the process all over again.

I always sought to cognitively understand where the problem rested so that I could find a way to solve it. And that's how I became a problem solver.

Obviously, today I know that from my perspective of being good at solving problems, what could I create? More problems that would validate that point of view.

Everything I had been trying, I also implemented in my professional work, so I decided to get educated in other practices that complemented Osteopathy, to understand how the mind works, how personality and behavior patterns are shaped. All these tools lent me very valuable information. When I integrated Access tools, I saw fast-tracked results in myself and in the people that I attended to. Something that caught my attention.

Everything I did for the people I treated at the time, gave them good results; they felt better, but after a few weeks or months, the symptoms returned. Do you know why? Because their physical condition had changed, but their point of view on a certain area of their life or a certain circumstance didn't. Therefore, their brain looked for ways to reorganize their body to "defend" itself against that circumstance or adapt to that environment once again.

During a regular working day at my center, a patient invited me to an Access Bars® class. At the time, I was pursuing my specialty in Osteopathy and didn't take the class; this was in 2016.

Days went by, and another person invited me again: « Juanjo, a friend of mine is hosting a Bars clinic, come try it. » This time, out of curiosity, I attended with two other people.

After the session, I didn't feel anything (or so I thought). I was calmer, but nothing more. One of the people who accompanied me (whom we'll call Maria) got up from the stretcher, devastated. She was crying, as if she was having a panic attack. The person who conducted the session approached Bruno and asked for contribution. That was the first time I was seeing Bruno work his magic. Bruno told Maria, "Don't think, just perceive," and continued, "Body, give me a yes," and Maria's body moved. "Body, give me a no," and her body moved in another direction.

Bruno asked her, "Truth, is this yours?" and her body moved in the direction that showed "no." "Do you want to return it to sender?" he asked. She said yes. Bruno said some strange words, Maria calmed down, her body relaxed, and we left.

Immediately after getting into the car, she fell completely asleep. When we arrived at Maria's house, I asked her, "How are you feeling?" "Strange," she replied, "something has lifted. I feel lighter, but I miss what I felt before."

Time went by, and I continued my lane with Osteopathy and my podcast, but what Bruno did with María remained in my mind. Thus, in 2022, I invited Bruno to participate in Quebrando Cascarones.

During the interview, I realized we had a lot of similarities in some concepts. So, I asked him for a session. (I spoke about this in the introduction to the book.) Once we finished, he suggested to me: Get your Bars run.

And this is where the questioning and this book began.

If you'd like to watch the podcast episode of that interview, I leave you the link.

1.2 But what is this?

I have to know.

"It is the curtains we create that block the intangible qualities of our lives, instead of seeking for the Light, we need to remove the curtains that prevent us from seeing it".
Rav Berg.

I listened to Bruno and took a Bars session.

A constant in my life was that my head seemed like a meeting room, a consortium of at least seven voices, constantly talking to me: "Do this; no, not this; better not do anything; or rather, let's call this person to see if they can do it."

I overthought all day, every day, and in the end, I didn't do anything.

After that Bars session, for the first time in my life, I didn't hear those voices in my head; that day I discovered silence.

A feeling of lightness, tranquility, and peace of mind is how I would describe it. And the best part was that I continued to have that feeling for 15 days.

By then, I meditated every morning, something that was a challenge for me: focusing on my breathing and connecting with the present moment. Suddenly, another transformative experience, doing my meditations was so easy and so satisfying that I became intrigued and then surged the question, "What is this?"

It was so profound and so beautiful the change I had, that a week later I took my first Access Bars class. I did it for two reasons:

1. Because I loved the results and wanted to share them.

2. Because I wanted to understand what the Bars were and how they worked.

The first reason was attained, the second was NOT, at that moment, and I say this because instead of finding an answer, I left with more doubts and more questions than what I had at the beginning. So, I took a second and third class.

The third was the global Access Bars class facilitated by Dr. Dain Heer. I loved the way Dain facilitated the class, and at that moment, I made another wonderful choice. I was going to be a Bars facilitator.

I became certified as an Access Bars Facilitator (BF), but the queries about how this wonderful world worked remained in me.

Now I could, not only give sessions, but I could also teach this technique. As I facilitated one class after another and another, the responses poured in. I became increasingly clear about the "why" of the magic of Access and the very fast change.

And the thing is that each tool contributes to changing the focus of areas of our brain that are responsible for survival.

I began facilitating my classes, relying on concepts from osteopathy and neuroscience, playing between the biological and the energetic.

One day I mentioned to Bruno how brain structures are very easily modulated using Access tools, and he said, "You have to write a book about this." And here it is.

Before moving on to your brain, for educational purposes, I'm going to give you a concept of energy: "It is the capacity of the basic unit of matter (atom) to perform a work, produce changes, or transform."

A movement is energy, a clap and its sound are energy, a yawn is energy, the sound you emit with a word is energy—basically, everything is energy. Just as Nikola Tesla said, *"To understand the universe, you must think in terms of energy, frequency, and vibration."*

And that includes human beings.

2
Getting to know your brain.

2.1 The three in one brain.

Where reacting, feeling and thinking get together.

"The brain weighs only about a kilo and a half, yet it is the most complex object in the solar system".
Michio Kaku.

The three-brain theory was proposed by neuroscientist Paul MacLean in the 1960s [(1)], in a model that seeks to explain the structure and function of the human brain through an evolutionary perspective. This theory suggests that our brain is not a homogeneous entity but rather is composed of three separate structures that have evolved at different stages in the history of our species. These three brains are:

1. The Reptilian Brain - Instinctive.
2. The Mammalian Brain - Emotional.
3. The New Brain - Intellectual.

Each of these parts has specific characteristics and functions, and together they amalgamate the complexity of our emotions, thoughts, and behaviors.

1. The Reptilian Brain

This is the oldest and most primitive part of our brain; it developed hundreds of millions of years ago. It is located at the base of the brain and is composed primarily of the brainstem and the cerebellum. This structure is responsible for the most basic and essential functions for survival, such as the regulation of breathing, heart rate, and primal instincts.

Main Functions:

- Survival instincts: Controls behaviors such as aggression, dominance, territoriality, and reproduction.
- Automatic responses: These include instinctive reactions to danger, such as the fight, flight, or freeze response.

This part of the brain operates automatically and unconsciously, meaning that many of our most basic reactions are the result of its activity. This is very likely where distracting implants are stored.

2. The Mammalian Brain.

Also known as the "emotional brain," this is the second layer that developed during evolution. This structure, named the Limbic System, is located in the middle of the brain and is composed of several regions, including the hippocampus, amygdala, and hypothalamus. The limbic system is essential for emotional regulation and founding memories.

Main Functions:

- Emotions: Processes feelings such as fear, anger, joy, and sadness.
- Memory: Plays a crucial role in creating long-term memories and associating emotional experiences to these memories.
- Social connections: Enables social interaction and empathy, influencing our relationships with others.

This part of the brain is essential for our capability to feel and emotionally connect with the world. Most likely, this is also where we create and sustain the foundations of our lives, since an important part of this brain is responsible for instant gratification.

3. The New Brain.

Its name is the Cerebral Cortex or Neocortex. It is the most recent and advanced part of the brain, and it developed primarily in mammals, and is responsible for our higher cognitive functions. This region is responsible for processes such as thinking, planning, language, and decision-making.

Main Functions:

- Critical thinking and problem-solving: It allows us to analyze complex situations and make informed decisions. « Something that apparently doesn't work very well for us. »
- Language and communication: It facilitates the ability to speak, write, and understand language.
- Creativity and abstraction: It is responsible for our ability to imagine, create, and think abstractly.

The cerebral cortex allows us to interact with the world in a "conscious" and reflective approach; it is crucial to our identity and personality. Here we store all the judgments and points of view that create our reality from what is known to us, from the good and the bad. From everything that has a concept, a form, and a structure in our world.

Based on this, we learned we must solve everything just by thinking.

Integration of The Three Brains

The three-brain theory suggests that these structures don't act in separate ways, but rather interact constantly and as needed, in a hierarchical order. For example:

I'm distractedly crossing a street with the cell phone in my hand. A car approaches and honks its horn. My response will be INSTINCTIVE

(Reptilian Brain): run or die. I don't need my cerebral cortex to reason "The car will hit me too hard, and the impact will injure me."

Another example: if I meet someone at a party who catches my attention, my Limbic Brain will react and create hormones that signal to my body that she's the chosen one for "something more." My response will be EMOTIONAL first, and then INTELLECTUAL: How do I approach her and win her over? I don't need that my INSTINCT jumps over to her to fulfill the premise of species preservation at that moment.

Implications of the Theory

When I learned about and studied this theory, I got aware that health and well-being cannot be approached by treating only the body or only the psyche. If we don't recognize ourselves as a whole being, we will spend our entire lives reacting and surrendering our state of mind to each and every thing "that happens to us"—I put that in quotes because nothing happens to you, you choose everything. « We'll talk about that later ».

This is where this book begins to gain shape because, often, our choices aren't really choices at all; they are reactions from our instinctive brain, being responses to what we feel, orchestrated by the instinctive brain associated to an emotion. Or they are outdated conclusions that we store in our intellectual brain.

Neuroscientist John-Dylan Haynes and his colleagues at the Max Planck Institute for Human Cognition and Brain in Germany conducted a study that addresses the idea that much of our choice-making is unconscious. The study, titled "Unconscious determinants of free decisions in the human brain," was published in the journal Nature Neuroscience in 2008. [(2)]

The primary goal of the study was to investigate the role of unconscious brain activity in decision-making. The researchers wanted to understand to what extent our choices are the result of conscious processes and to what extent they are influenced by unconscious factors.

Participants in the study were placed in a functional magnetic resonance imaging (fMRI) scanner while they performed a task in which they had to freely decide when to press a button. Throughout the experiment, the scientists monitored the subjects' brain activity, focusing on areas of the brain associated with decision-making.

The results showed that brain activity related to the decision to press the button could be predicted 5 to 10 seconds before the action. This suggests that choices can be initiated by unconscious processes, implying that occasionally our choices are not as "free" as we think. The study concluded that approximately 95% of our decisions are the result of automatic and unconscious processes.

This finding has profound implications for our understanding of free will and personal responsibility. If a large part of our decisions are made without conscious awareness, it means that most of our choices are based on learned or implanted programming.

Many of these choices are made based on the sensations perceived in the body, and many of them from the heaviness of a history stored for survival, which is not necessarily our present context.

2.2 The Neural Pathway.

The internal wiring system that connects everything.

"Evolution is marked by moments of Kensho and Satori".
Kitaro Nishida.

The human brain is an incredibly complex structure, composed by thousands of millions of neurons that communicate with each other through connections called synapses. These connections form what we know as neural pathways.

Understanding how these pathways are formed is essential to comprehend how we learn, remember, and respond to our environment. This information is important because, when using Access tools, you will modulate and change your brain and its functioning by updating your neural pathways.

These pathways are truly networks of neurons that fire together every time we perform an action, think about something, or feel an emotion. Every time we use our three brains, together or separately. The more times a neural pathway is activated, the stronger that connection becomes.

An important function for creating these neural pathways is ***Perception***, which presents itself as follows:

There are two types of perceptions.

First-order perception is that which is categorized as an irrefutable type of truth. For example, if I hold an apple in my hand and show it to you, my perception and yours will be: It's an apple. This is a truth for both of us, and it is almost always supported by the information we obtain through our five senses.

Second-order perception is that which passes through the filter of each person's interpretation, which is created through each individual's experiences and concepts. For example, continuing with the apple example, I may think the apple is sweet, but for you it isn't. For you the apple may be a fruit with a soft texture, but for me it may be the opposite.

Another example might be if I show you a twenty-dollar bill, for both of us, it's a billet (first-order perception), but for you, it might be too much, too little, or even worthless because it's not your currency (second-order perception).

Formation of Neural Pathways through Shock

Shock, whether emotional or physical, has a profound impact on the foundation of neural pathways. When we experience an unexpected or traumatic event, our brain reacts intensely.

For these types of experiences to form a neural pathway, the activation of the limbic system (emotional brain) is necessary.

How does this process work? A shock is any situation that arises unexpectedly, classified by our brain as something life-threatening and before which we are alone. This cataloging relies largely on the Brain Stem (Reptilian Brain), which is responsible for activating correct and effective automatic responses, which have worked to survive. This is confirmed by John-Dylan Haynes's study.

Likewise, this cataloging is based on first- and second-order perception. The Neocortex (Intellectual Brain) is responsible for sustaining this second-order perception over time. Something that can be called a Presumptive Reality.

Let me explain with an example: I'm taking a car ride and suffer a terrible accident that almost costs me my life (bumps, bruises, cuts, and fractures). There's nothing to interpret here. My Reptilian brain will make the corresponding association: "cars kill". So, every time I get into a car, when I see one of that color, that brand, or every time I pass by that place, my brain will activate the fight-or-flight state to be ready.

Let's talk about Association. It's the connection your brain makes to keep track of what it feels internally and links it with the first thing it perceives from the outside. Most of these ***Associations*** are stored in the Amygdala.

Another very clear example is this. A newborn baby feels cared for, protected, and nourished by its mother while it feeds and feels her chest; it is its safe place. Suddenly, the day arrives to get a vaccine, and the mother is told, "Place the baby on your breast," and suddenly the child is hit with the shock of the prick. What once gave it security and protection, now feels like pain and discomfort. At that moment, the baby has created an association with breast milk: "This taste (first-order perception received through the sense of taste) felt unpleasant and painful (second-order perception). Therefore, now I reject it." This is what we know as Lactose Intolerance.

Formation of Neural Pathways through Repetition

Repetition is another powerful mechanism for forming neural pathways, essential in learning and motor skills. The more we repeat an action or idea, the stronger the connection becomes. How does this process work? It consists of two fundamental parts: *Consolidation* and *Automation*.

To ride a bicycle, you initially think about how to balance yourself, how to steer the wheel, how to pedal, until there comes a time when this entire process ***Consolidates*** and becomes one. The repetition of this series of consolidated movements leads to ***Automation***. At this point, you no longer think, you just do it. Once you ride a bicycle, you hop on and control it without thinking. And this is precisely an example of the creation of a neural network through repetition.

This mechanism we use to learn to ride a bicycle is the same one we use to create a response to a shock. A person who beginning to smoke, must think through all the steps at first: lighting the cigarette, bringing it to their mouth, and inhaling the smoke. After a couple of days of repetition, it will become an automatic practice. It's based on the association "the cigarette makes me feel...".

The Interaction between Shock and Repetition

It's interesting to notice that shock and repetition are not mutually exclusive processes; they often interact. An emotionally shocking event can motivate a person not to repeat a behavior to avoid the same situation in the future.

Imagine this. Your father has just taken out a loan to buy a house. Suddenly, he is laid off from his job (first-order perception). His interpretation of this situation may be "I won't have any money" (second-order perception). The brain needs to respond to the shock of this unexpected and dramatic situation.

During this process, you may hear concepts like: "There isn't enough money," "If I don't work, I won't have any money," "Only when I get a job will I have money."

Ask: Have you created a neural pathway through repetition with money and made these ideas your own?

These phrases and information became associated with feelings of anxiety, fear, insecurity, and lack. Guess what you're going to want to avoid in your future?

This was put to test by a team of researchers at New York University, led by neuroscientist Robert M. Sapolsky and other collaborators. [3]

The researchers exposed rats (Rattus norvegicus) to the smell of cherry blossoms while giving them a mild electric shock. After several repetitions, the rats associated the smell with the electric shock, showing a fear response to it. The goal of the study was to demonstrate the transmission of information within the genetic material of the offspring (or from parents to children in the case of humans). So, after subjecting the rats to these stimuli, their reproduction was tested.

The result was that the offspring that had never been exposed to the smell of cherry blossoms or electric shocks showed a fear response upon merely perceiving the smell.

This indicated that the parents' experience had influenced the offspring's behavior.

Researchers suggest that this phenomenon could be related to epigenetic changes, which are modifications in genetic expression that do not alter the DNA sequence.

According to Dr. Theresa Bullard, a pioneer in the dissemination and experimentation of topics that merge spirituality, quantum physics, and science, 85% of the genetic information in our DNA chain is unquantified. This 85% stores all this information, which we could call behavioral patterns acquired through inheritance.

This type of research has opened new opportunities for understanding how parents' experiences influence the biology and behavior of their offspring.

Obviously, you will also create neural pathways that have a pleasant (rewarding) association in your body, such as your first kiss or receiving your first paycheck. These neural pathways are what create our limits and boundaries, driven by concepts like, "That kiss was the best thing that ever happened to me," "I have enough money, now I can be happy." These limits lead us in search of what is known.

2.3 The Brain Waves.

It's not about quantity, it's about quality.

"The mind is your best ally or your worst enemy".
Marianne Williamson.

Did you know that the human brain can generate approximately 20 watts of electricity even at rest?

This energy is modulated according to the number of responses your brain produces to different stimuli.

Imagine this: in your living room, you have an electrical outlet that only powers the television. In the kitchen, another outlet powers the blender, the refrigerator, and the coffee maker.

Which one do you think carries more electrical energy?

This is how your brain works: the more simultaneous processes it performs, the greater its electrical activity.

Your brain receives information and processes it through electrical waves that are transmitted primarily through the thalamocortical networks (related to the mammalian brain), structures which integrate the body's sensations.

Then, the cortical neurons of the so-called new brain take that information and prepare the body's responses.

I won't go into the mechanisms of action or neurochemical processes; I just want you to understand the frequencies at which the brain functions and what happens at each of them.

Beta (13–30 Hz)

Typical state of wakefulness, alertness, active attention, logical thinking, problem-solving; increased activity during preparatory motor tasks and execution.

The person remains in a state of alert, focus, and analytical processing. It is sometimes observed that excessive increases in beta can be related to anxiety or hyperactivity; decreases in beta can occur during relaxation or sustained distraction.

Alpha (8–13 Hz)

Typical state of relaxation with closed eyes, gentle vigilance; inhibition of irrelevant sensory processing to avoid distractions.

The person enters a state of cortical "cooling down," which inhibits overstimulation and increases the efficiency of internal processing when directing attention to a goal. When in alpha, the body's repair processes occur, as the system exits the state of reactivity.

Theta (4–8 Hz)

Typical state of somnolence, sleep-wake transition; during tasks involving spatial and working memory and exploration of new contexts; a state associated with meditators who are in deep relaxation.

The person has access to their intuition, memory retrieval, prospecting, and planning for certain tasks. Here, the person is more self-confident, knowing that their intuition and knowledge are a powerful guide, and they have access to their creativity.

Delta (0.5–4 Hz)

Typical state: deep slow-wave sleep; also occurs in states of anesthesia or some phases of cognitive incoherence.

The person experiences a reduction in voluntary attention and individual conscious processing; in sleep, the body enters a state of physiological repair and restoration. There is a sense of trust and integration with all that exists. People describe this state as oneness.

Let's return to the example of the electrical outlet: the more your focus is external, the more electrical current you need. Therefore, you are in Beta, a state in which everything that happens has an external cause: the government, family, politics, children. There are so many stimuli that you remain reactive and constantly on alert, trying to resolve everything that happens in your environment, yet nothing changes because your attention is outside. You are like the electrical outlet in the kitchen.

When you reduce your brain activity, you lower your frequency to Alpha. This is where your attention turns inward, you become more introspective, and you start to analyze why things appear in your reality. This is where you begin to take responsibility for your life, your actions, and your choices.

In Theta, you have already transcended matter and begin to focus on energy. Techniques like Theta Healing seek to bring the person to these states, in which tissue repair, regulation of organic functions, and reorganization of thought contribute to the transformation of the body. Energy influences matter.

But you can go further. Delta is the state where you no longer find separation between matter and energy. You know that matter is made of energy and that you can alter matter by changing the energy that composes it. And that includes you. You know that your vibration is the outlet that powers what you see in your reality. By changing your vibration and your attention, you change what you see in your reality as matter.

All these waves reflect the person's state of consciousness; the slower the waves, the more conscious you are being.

One of the most unique contributions to the understanding of consciousness in Latin America comes from the Mexican psychophysiologist Jacobo Grinberg-Zylberbaum (1946–disappeared in 1994). His proposal, known as the Sintergy Theory, attempts to explain how the perception of reality is generated from the interaction between the brain and a fundamental energy field.

In this model, Grinberg proposed the existence of the neuronal field, understood as a macro-energy distortion originating from the micro-distortions produced by neurons and their connections. This field interacts with a deeper structure of space, which he called the Lattice or holographic network, thus generating interference patterns that become the basis of conscious experience.

If you don't understand anything by now, let me summarize it for you: the distortions of your brain and mind will be reflected in your reality. In other words: ***Your point of view creates your reality.***

According to Grinberg [4], the sum of all individual neuronal fields would give rise to a hyperfield, a collective field of information that would enable phenomena of interconnection between consciousnesses. Although the scientific community has questioned its approaches due to a lack of scientific evidence, the Sintergy Theory represents a pioneering attempt to build bridges between neuroscience, quantum physics, and Mexican shamanic traditions.

Let me try to explain it to you again: lower brain waves correspond to higher states of consciousness. A faster wave is perceived as separate; a slower wave is perceived as unity. And the set of these waves creates what Carl Jung called the Collective Unconscious. We are creating this reality together, and everything we see in the world as reality is a projection of a micro-universe within our brains.

3
Brain-hacking and Biology.

3.1 Tools and Structures.

Potentializing your brain regions.

"The human brain is design to fight for survival".
Francisco Mora.

Before we begin, please don't undermine your brain. This beautiful and enigmatic organ is full of structures and functions that have as a premise human survival. So, if you're reading these pages, congratulations! It's a success for your brain. You're alive, and that's what matters.

Remember that your brain is the product of thousands of years of evolution; it has evolved from escaping tigers and predators to online shopping and avoiding making paychecks at the end of the month. The stimuli are different, and the resources and structures you use are the same.

So, once again, I ask you not to undermine your brain, because its original design is focused on the survival of the species, not on being happy, not on having the life of your dreams. It's simply survival.

What is the richness in Access tools? They help you get out of a survival mode and start functioning with your brain on a different programming. One that allows you to live the life you choose to create, not the one you've been given.

In this section, I'll detail some Access tools you can use every day, and I'll relate them to the areas of your brain you're influencing by using them.

So, buckle up, and let's begin the most fun part of this journey: uncovering and discovering your full potential.

3.2 Mirror Neurons.

Who does this belong to?®

"A child doesn't learn what you tell him, a child learns what they see in their caregivers".
Rosario Dominguez.

Has it ever happened to you that you're watching a very romantic movie and cry because the protagonist dies and the love never comes true? Or in the middle of a chase scene, your hands start to sweat, and your heart starts to race?

You've gotten into the role. But how? Easy, your brain has the ability to do it, and it's not something very voluntary that you can control.

In the 1990s, a team of researchers at the University of Parma, Italy, led by Giacomo Rizzolatti, discovered mirror neurons. (5)

Obviously, the discovery was purely coincidental and, one might even say, a mistake. These neurons are found mainly in areas of the brain related to motor skills, such as the premotor cortex, on the side of the forehead.

Mirror neurons are activated in an individual's brain when observing or perceiving another person performing an action. And how did they come to be discovered?

During his studies with chimpanzees at the University of Parma, Giacomo was monitoring the chimpanzee's brain areas to understand whether the same areas as in humans were activated depending on the stimulus presented.

During his break, he went to the other side of the room where the study was being conducted and was able to observe that the brain areas related to chewing, swallowing, and jaw movements were lighting up on the computer. Surprise, the chimpanzee was copying what Giacomo was doing, and all of this was involuntary.

They conducted further studies to identify the functions related to these neurons and discovered that they were not only activated by motor stimuli, but also by the perception of sensations such as cold, emotions such as fear or anger, and they also activate when sensing pain.

After conducting all these studies on the chimpanzee brains, it was time to put them to the test in humans; this had to be investigated. Of course, before this research, we never realized that when someone yawns, they "yawn contagiously." We also didn't realize that when we feed a baby and tell them to open their mouth, we find ourselves with our mouths open and "passing" the food the baby is eating. But science is science, and it had to be investigated. The result was that, yes, humans also have mirror neurons.

I present to you this wonderful Access tool: Who does this belong to? A question as simple as it is effective that will change your reality.

One of the reasons I decided to study Physiotherapy and Osteopathy was because I had the "ability" to feel other people's pain. When someone came to a session, I would ask them, "Does it hurt here?" And I would touch them in the exact place where it hurt.

Then I understood that my ability is nothing more than a lot of presence with my body, my mirror neurons in action, perceiving other people's pain.

When I read about mirror neurons, I began to question whether this ability was a function that all people have.

How much of the pains you are perceiving in your body don't belong to you? How much of the fatigue and stress you are perceiving in your body don't belong to you? Would you like to return everything to its origin, please? ***Who does this belong to?***

Your mirror neurons are designed to imitate the behaviors of others. In the movie Tarzan, this guy uses his mirror neurons to move like an ape, because when he does, he's part of the pack, to satisfy one of our brain's basic needs: BELONGING. If you notice it's an instinct for survival, now the question is: Do you really need to belong? Do you really need to fit in? How many of the thoughts, patterns, and behaviors you have daily aren't yours, and do you use them only to fit in and belong? ***Who does this belong to?***

Question this for a moment: If your family always had money problems, always used debt as their only resource to acquire goods, if in a conversation you've always heard things like: "money corrupts people," "just because someone has money that makes them arrogant," "money is the root of all evil," how much of your financial reality doesn't belong to you? How many of your financial "problems" are you creating to belong to your clan? ***Who does this belong to?***

When you ask, "***Who does this belong to?***" you invite your brain to question, "Is this really mine?" What your brain will do is evaluate the neural pathway that connects that record to that function or reaction in your body, to modulate it.

Now guess what? 92% of the concepts that are "yours" you learned from someone else, unconsciously. The remaining 8% you also learned from someone else, but in a more conscious way.

The first group includes all the things you saw, heard, and perceived that had a chemical impact on your body (the situation was attached to an emotion). The second group includes situations like religion, a soccer team, political ideology, etc., which fall under the concept of family heritage.

A little more about my story. In that first facilitation session with Bruno, I clearly remember him asking me:

If you could take anything from this session, what would it be? I asked for coherence. During the session, he asked a few questions, until we arrived at this basic resource on which I was building my relationship with money.

My parents divorced when I was 3 years old. One of the reasons this happened was because there were always money problems, there was never enough. My father couldn't make ends meet at his jobs, my mother couldn't make enough money from the business, and that was the theme of every night.

My interpretation of what I saw and that no one told me was: Money causes fights, conflicts, and separation. What was the best strategy I had to avoid fights, conflicts, and separation in my life? Not having money.

And with this little anecdote, you can realize how interesting it can be for your life to always ask yourself, ***"Who does this belong to?".*** Your mirror neurons copied it at some point, and if that action is attached to an emotion, it becomes a survival resource for you.

Every time a thought comes to your head, ask, ***"Who does this belong to?".***

Every time you're in line at the grocery store and "feel" pressured and in lack, ask, ***"Who does this belong to?".***

Every time you go out on the street and start to feel fear, ask, ***"Who does this belong to?".***

An additional tip to change the function of your mirror neurons: Change the word "feel" or "have" to "perceive."

Instead of saying "I'm afraid," you can start saying "I'm perceiving fear." This will prevent your brain from making those other people's feelings, thoughts, and emotions your own.

3.3 Ascending Reticular Activating System (ARAS).

What else is possible?® / How does it get better than this?®

> *"Where you put your attention, you put your energy".*
> *Joe Dispenza.*

We all have that neighbor in our community who spends all day at her window watching what's happening on the block. She's the one who knows all the latest news. She's known as the neighborhood gossip, whom we'll call Mrs. Ara for didactic purposes.

The Ascending Reticular Activating System (ARAS) is a network of neurons that extends from the brainstem (reptilian brain) to the cortical areas of the brain (new brain). This system plays a crucial role in regulating attention, wakefulness, and alert status. It's the structure that allows us to focus and pay attention to things, using neurotransmitters such as norepinephrine (to reduce states of stress), serotonin (to regulate states of mood and sleep), and acetylcholine (responsible for attention and memory formation).

This Mrs. Ara is in charge of showing you pregnant women when you're thinking about having a baby and you cross paths on the street with all the pregnant women in the city, and no, it's not that they all agreed to take a stroll in front of you.

It's the same one that finds out you want to buy a car, from a certain brand and color, and shows you all the cars of that make and color. It's your ARA(S) in charge, constantly saying, "Look, look, look..."

What happens in your brain when it's time to make the house payments? And you tell yourself, "I won't be able to pay." Your ARA(S) kicks in and shows you that reality. It's going to show you everything it can to reinforce that idea you just had, "I won't be able to."

When night falls, you stand in front of your bathroom mirror, look at the small wrinkle on your forehead, and focus your attention on that detail. What your ARA(S) does is tell you: "Now look at the bags under your eyes, look at how little hair you have, look at this blemish." And so, without noticing it, you'll have fallen into a spiral that will begin to show you whatever you're focusing your attention on.

In 1995, Vladimir Poponin and Peter Gariaev, together with the Russian Academy of Sciences, conducted a study to determine the behavior of human DNA in the presence of photon particles [(6)], a highly rigorous study in which they even limited the air inside the chambers to create a vacuum and eliminate inertia.

By measuring the photons, they observed that they were distributed in a dispersed and chaotic manner. The next step was to place human DNA and observe what happened. What happened was that the photons clustered neatly around the DNA strand.

When the DNA was removed from the tube, the photons were expected to uncluster and disorganize again. But that didn't happen. They remained grouped together even though the DNA was gone, leading to the conclusion that human DNA has an impact on the environment.

This study explains two things: the first is our ability to perceive when "something" has happened in a place—when you arrive and feel anger, discomfort, or sadness, to name a few examples. You don't know what happened in that place, but your body can perceive it. And the second is that your mere presence can change your entire environment.

Let me tell you a story.

I traveled to Quito to attend a concert with my family, and I had booked the hotel in advance. When we arrived, my body felt a certain discomfort, which could be described as anxiety.

I approached the counter, and the manager asked me for my reservation information. He entered the information into his computer, asked for a few minutes, and left. Immediately afterward, the sensation in my body became more intense. At that moment, I began repeating in my mind the Access tools, ***"What else is possible?"*** *and* ***"How does it get better than this?"*** I did this several times until the sensation in my body dissipated.

The manager returned, and the sensation reappeared. By that time, I was aware that I was sensing the discomfort of the man serving me. So, I just continued the exercise in my mind, ***"What else is possible and how does it get better than this?".*** And once again, the man left.

When he returned, he said, "Mr. Suarez, there was a problem with your reservation. The room you requested is not available." To which I replied, "Well, how does it get better than this?" The man kindly said, "I have requested a suite for your stay, and we will keep the price of the double room you had reserved."

What I'm getting at with this anecdote:

1. If you are present with the energy being shown, you have the ability to recognize what's contracting you. If it's not yours, you can give it back (Who does this belong to? The previous tool).
2. If you align or react to a "complex" situation, you will create more of that contracting energy. But if you acknowledge it and open yourself to new possibilities by asking, ***"What else is possible and how does it get better than this?"***, you will create more space for something different to show.
3. Transform your ARAS from a problem observer to a possibility magnet. How? With a simple but effective question: ***What else is possible and how does it get better than this?***

But what does this question do to your brain that transforms you into a possibility magnet? When you ask your brain ***"What else is possible and how does it get better than this?"*** And you lower the hormonal load of what you're feeling in the body, you're literally fragmenting the Intellectual and Instinctive Brain, because you're working on the bridge that unites them, which is Emotion.

Instead of focusing your ARA(S) on the conflict and the corresponding reaction, your brain will begin to search, analyze, and create new neural pathways in search of possibilities to resolve it.

The complete opposite happens when your attention is focused on the problem or a fixed point of view that doesn't allow you to see beyond it, since you're giving it your full attention.

For example, if your point of view is that your partner doesn't love you enough because they don't give you shoes, you'll overlook it when they give you flowers, chocolates, when they invite you out to dinner, or when they shower you with kisses and hugs, because your attention is focused on "they don't give me shoes."

This was tested in a study called "Selective Attention and Inattentional Blindness," conducted by Daniel Simons and Christopher Chabris in 1999.

Selective attention is a cognitive phenomenon that allows human beings to focus on relevant information while ignoring irrelevant stimuli. « Which, incidentally, are filtered by each person's perception and perspective ».

This study not only shed light on the nature of attention but also revealed the surprising limitations of our perception.

In the experiment, participants were exposed to a video in which... No, wait, would you like to be part of the experiment?

Scan the code and follow the video instructions. Let's test you, let's see which group you belong to. Please don't judge yourself. It's just a game. Go watch the video, I'll be waiting for you.

Ready? how did it go?

Let me tell you that the results of the study surprised the researchers, as 50% of the participants didn't notice anything at all, meaning they had developed this phenomenon called "inattentional blindness," which refers to an individual's inability to perceive stimuli present in the environment while concentrating on a specific task.

This finding suggests that attention is not a passive process; it is actually an active mechanism for filtering relevant information from irrelevant information.

Simons and Chabris's research was published in the journal Perception (7) and has become a benchmark in the fields of cognitive psychology and neuroscience.

The study also raises profound questions about the nature of perception and conscious experience. How many important stimuli do we miss in our daily lives due to selective attention and fixed perspectives?

How much do you limit the creation of your life by focusing on problem-solving? Do you dare to focus your attention by using ***What else is possible, and how does it get better than this?***

3.4 Amygdala.

Everything is the opposite of what it appears to be, and nothing is the opposite of what it appears to be.

"If you can look at a tree without any picture, without any knowledge, then the observer is the observed object".

Jiddu Krishnamurti.

The amygdala is like a bean-sized black box in our brain. Located in the brain's limbic system, it plays a crucial role in regulating emotions and fear response.

The amygdala is located deep within the temporal lobes, in both hemispheres of the brain. It's situated near the hippocampus, another key structure in memory and learning.

The amygdala is made up of several nuclei, each with specific functions that connect to different brain regions, allowing for the complex integration of emotional information. To make it easier to locate, imagine your two ears being held together by a string with a knot in the middle—that's where it is.

An experiment on its role in trauma processing and storage was conducted by Joseph LeDoux and his team in the 1990s. This work has been fundamental to understanding how the amygdala is involved in the emotional response to fear and trauma.

The aim of the study was to investigate how the amygdala processes fear and how emotional memories associated with traumatic experiences are formed. LeDoux used an experimental approach involving rats.

In his experiments, he exposed the rats to a neutral sound (such as a tone) paired with a mild electric shock. After several repetitions, the rats learned to associate the sound with the pain of the electric shock, showing a fear response to the sound even when the shock was not presented.

By observing the brain activity of rats, LeDoux and his team concluded that the amygdala is crucial for learning and associative memory related to fear.

When the rats' amygdala was damaged, they did not show the fear response to sound, confirming that this brain structure is responsible for processing and storing emotional memories related to traumatic experiences.

LeDoux's findings have been published in several scientific journals over the years, including papers in Nature and the Journal of Neuroscience. [8]

This work has had enormous implications for understanding trauma-related disorders, such as post-traumatic stress disorder (PTSD).

LeDoux's research suggests that the amygdala is not only involved in the immediate response to danger, but also in the formation of memories.

The amygdala is primarily known for its role in the emotional response to fear. However, its functions also include:

1. Evaluating threats and activating fight-or-flight responses.
2. It participates in the management of other emotions such as anger, sadness, and joy.
3. Stores memories associated with emotions, which influences in how we respond to similar situations in the future.
4. Identifies other people's emotions, facilitating social communication.

If you're familiar with other Access tools, the amygdala is basically responsible for supporting *the Big 5 and the zero-sum game of reality.* If you're not familiar, I highly recommend you to take an Access Bars Class to understand more of this concepts.

The amygdala stores experiences to prevent future catastrophic scenarios (the Big 5's Presumptive Realities). When faced with the perception of danger, it chooses the most effective resource or program for survival (the Big 5's Need of Reactive Realities), and generates associations with the environment, clothing, objects, sounds, etc. (the Big 5's Need of Reactive Response Systems). Together with the ARAS, they direct your focus to everything that puts you at risk (the Big 5's Artificial Intelligence Actualizers), and not only you, but also the clan to which you belong (the Big 5's Fifth Element). What's all this for? To remain in the safe zone (Zero-Sum game of reality) which price is paid with discomfort, inconvenience and unhappiness.

Here are some examples:

You are currently 7 years old. You walk into the kitchen for the first time and place your hand on the hot pan. Your amygdala has just registered; this burns. Conclusion: Don't touch the hot pan, so as not to put your body at risk.

You are now 16 years old and in your first relationship. You are having a wonderful time, and one day you discover that your partner is cheating because he or she is dating someone else. At that moment, your amygdala kicks in and once again forms a conclusion: People can't be trusted.

If you notice, the amygdala is responsible for drawing conclusions and assessing future dangers based on lived experiences. What to do? Draw your amygdala's conclusions. How? With Access's crazy phrase: ***Everything is the opposite of what it appears to be, and nothing is the opposite of what it appears to be.***

But it's a phrase that doesn't say anything, you might think. It's like doing this: 1 + -1 = 0. Adding a positive and a negative together is the same as nothing. Exactly!

Do you understand now? When a thought overwhelms you, you can use this tool:

Take that thought and first ask yourself if it's yours. If it isn't, you know what to do.

If it does belong to you, take the thought, focus on the sensation that occurs in your body, and repeat as many times as necessary: ***Everything is the opposite of what it appears to be, and nothing is the opposite of what it appears to be.***

Focus on the thought or the situation, but above all on the sensation in your body, repeat the phrase until the sensation changes completely. Can't sleep? Use this phrase instead of counting sheep. It's surprising the change this tool can bring to your body in terms of your relaxation and tranquility.

Returning to the example of your first relationship and that conclusion about trusting people, take the image, perceive the sensation in your body, and repeat: Everything is the opposite of what it appears to be , and nothing is the opposite of what it appears to be .

When you receive surprising news, like a payment you didn't expect, and you recognize a sensation in your body, try repeating first: ***Everything is the opposite of what it appears to be, and nothing is the opposite of what it appears to be.*** Before asking, ***"What else is possible and how does it get better than this?"*** This way you will first deactivate the hormonal load in your body.

3.5 Nucleus Accumbens.

If I choose this, how will my life look in 5 years?

"Thoughts become things. If you can see it in your mind, you will have it in your hands".
Bob Proctor.

I don't know if the mind is actually where we see our thoughts, but if we can bring them to our Nucleus Accumbens, our body will begin to sense them and know where to take us.

In 2011, Alia Crum and her team at Yale University conducted a study exploring how visualization can influence the brain's perception and response. The study was called "The Effect of Expectation on Pain." [(9)]

One group visualized a pain treatment believed to be effective, while another group received no specific visualization instructions. The group that was instructed to visualize the treatment's effectiveness improved by 47% compared to the group that only took the medication.

Several studies have used neuroimaging techniques, such as functional magnetic resonance imaging (fMRI), to observe how the nucleus accumbens is activated during tasks involving reward visualization.

In 1998, Berridge and Robinson conducted research on how visualized reward expectations [(10)] influence learning and memory, highlighting the role of the nucleus accumbens in these processes.

In sports, it has been shown that visualization can improve performance and activate brain areas related to reward. A study by Cumming and Williams (2012) [(11)] analyzed how visualization techniques improve mobility and the execution of sports gestures in athletes.

My question is, is this in the mind, in memory, or is it a capacity of our brain? Previous studies have determined the importance of the nucleus accumbens in regards of the use of imagination and visualization.

Now, what about people who lack the ability to visualize (something called Aphantasia in Access). Are they destined to not recognize their future? No, using imagination isn't the only resource; you can also connect with sensations in your body.

Every time you ask yourself the Access question, ***"If I choose this, what will my life be like in 5 years?"*** this area of your brain activates and produces neurotransmitters that allow us to live the experience in the present moment. It's literally giving you the ability to travel through time and space.

That trip, how does it feel? That house, how does it feel? That relationship, how does it feel? Does it expand or contract you?

Do you remember the experiment where they showed that DNA influences the environment? We're going to use it again.

If you energetically know the sensation of what you want to actualize, when your DNA (body) perceives that familiar sensation in the environment, it will activate the nucleus accumbens to tell you: "This way, the reward is this way." Often, perceiving and following energy isn't linear; it's not a sequence of steps as we believe or think; it's a matter of being present with the energy of what you desire and making friends with the sensation in the present moment.

Here's another anecdote of mine.

I was very excited about taking the Access class Talk to the Entities . Every night I asked myself, ***"What will my life be like in 5 years if I take this class?"*** And the sensation that showed up in my body was very expansive and somewhat confusing. The class was approaching, and I couldn't seem to actualize the money for the class.

As always, I spoke to Bruno, and he contributed a couple of questions. One of them was: "What is required of you to actualize the money for the class?" And the first thing that came to mind was: "Play soccer." So that's what I did.

I called a friend and asked him to invite me to play that night. I went, and during the game, I felt like my body was back to that of a child, running excitedly after the ball. It was all fun and relaxing. I had a great time, so much so that I completely forgot about the class, the money, everything.

When the game ended, on my way home, I grabbed my phone and saw a message from someone saying, "Juanjo, I'm paying you for the 20 sessions I owed you." And that's how the money was actualized. Does that make sense? No. Did I work hard to generate that money? No. Does it seem like magic? Yes.

The invitation is to always, always, ask yourself this question: ***If I choose this, what will my life be like in 5 years?*** Because every time you ask it, the Nucleus Acumbens generates a chemical reaction in your body that you'll recognize when a possibility presents itself in your environment. You'll be opening the doors to infinite possibilities.

Now, what happens if you ask this question and notice a feeling of compression, heaviness, or stiffness in your body? Listen to that as well. Your body is more magical than you think, and it has amazing capabilities.

Let me tell you another anecdote. I was treating a friend who is a professional triathlete who competes all over the world. That session was part of her preparation for a competition in Mexico.

During the osteopathy session, I asked her: "How are you feeling about the competition?" She replied: "It's a bit strange. Every time I think about the competition, I get an uneasy feeling." I asked a couple of questions and was able to recognize that it wasn't a judgment or a point of view; she was aware of something.

I told her, "Maybe it would be better if you listen to yourself." To which she replied, "I can't. My participation is already confirmed, and besides, the coach is the one who decides, so we have to go."

She had chosen to go, despite her discomfort. What happened? She fell off her bike, tore her right thigh and suffered a muscle tear, had to stop for more than two months, had emergency costs, and a feeling of discomfort.

Use the sensation of light and heavy as a compass in your life; it will always lead you to a more expansive life.

Let me see if I can explain light and heavy with this metaphor. Imagine a hot air balloon stored in its bag, folded and squeezed until it barely takes up the space of a one-meter-by-one-meter box. In that state, it feels dense, compact, heavy. Now think about what happens when you unfold it and fill it with hot air: the balloon expands, takes up much more space, and, paradoxically, becomes light—so light that it can rise and fly.

This is how it works for us, too. When we contract, we often do so to fit in, to fit into a mold, to be accepted. But this contraction limits us: it reduces what we can be, know, receive, and perceive. On the other hand, when we seek our own lightness, we expand. We cease to be just matter and become space, energy, and consciousness. Lightness is, in essence, being more of you.

3.6 The hippocampus.

Interesting point of view, I have this point of view.

"If you think you can do it, you are in the right. If you think you can't, then you are also in the right".

Henry Ford.

To question a belief, you must remove its unquestionable status. Our brain has the ability to associate an event with the emotions and sensations perceived in the body, as I've already told you. When this happens in the form of a shock or is repeated several times, we have chemically and psychologically formed a belief.

This is processed in an area of the brain shaped like a seahorse, hence the name of the Hippocampus. It's an "S"-shaped structure located inside the brain, in an area called the temporal lobe, located on the sides of the head, just above the ears.

It's kind of like a "labyrinth" that is connected to many other parts of the brain, allowing it to receive and send important information.

Its main job is to help us create and store new memories, as well as evoke an experience, a place, or a conversation. It also plays an important role in tracing our surroundings and learning new things.

Without the hippocampus, it would be very difficult to form new memories or learn new skills.

During the night, these new memories become part of long-term memory. A memory that it fulfills the equation: event + emotion + sensation; it will no longer be just a memory.

For a belief to be sustained, it must have a particular characteristic; it is unquestionable, and the moment this happens, the emotion or sensation that sustains it appears in the body.

In his book The Spontaneous Healing of Belief, Gregg Braden tells the story of a woman whose husband lived under a deadly conviction: he believed that all the men in his family were destined to die at 35.

His grandfather, father, and brother had died exactly on his 35th birthday, and he was about to reach that age.

The expectation of death had become a kind of silent sentence that both awaited with dread.

Braden had the opportunity to work with the couple and delve deeper into the beliefs that sustained this family pattern.

During the process, they discovered that this idea was not just a thought, but an inherited survival program, engraved in the body and the unconscious.

Fear, anticipation, and emotional memory had created a biological reality: the body was preparing to die, because that's what it believed it should do.

By releasing the emotion associated with the belief (the sense of inevitable destiny, the fear of repeating family history), the body also changed.

When the mind stops sending danger signals, the nervous system stops responding with stress, and cells can return to their natural balance.

That's precisely what happened: the man lived past 35 with full vitality and no signs of disease.

This story profoundly illustrates how an unquestioned belief can become a biological command, and how, by transforming internal perception, the body responds with a new physiological reality.

Braden invites us to look beyond conscious thought: what we believe is possible or inevitable doesn't just reside in the mind but is imprinted on every cell in the body.

Access has a tool ***"interesting point of view I have this point of view"***. What happens in your brain when a belief becomes just a point of view? Something simple happens: questioning begins. What I believed and what was unquestionable now has the status of a point of view. And if it's just a point of view, there are probably other points of view.

If you've used this Access tool, you know that the change it brings is wonderful, lasting, and profound, and do you know why? Simple: you're canceling the body's chemical response, you're canceling the emotional reaction and sensation in the body, so your brain doesn't feel attacked and doesn't resist the change. Isn't that magical?

Try it, take something you believe in with complete conviction, and start.

Interesting point of view, I have that point of view that... now take the next one.

Interesting point of view, I have that point of view that... and the next one.

Interesting point of view, I have that point of view that... and the next one.

And so on, with everything, absolutely everything that comes to mind, until you run out of ideas. Once that happens, we will have dismantled a belief.

Doing this exercise allows you to recognize that this "belief" is just the tip of the iceberg, supported by a multitude of concepts, judgments, and points of view with which you have woven a web. This is why it's called a belief system.

Once you finish this exercise, or after using any of the tools I mentioned before, don't forget to use the one below to deepen the cleansing process you are doing.

3.7 Synaptic Pruning.

The Access Consciousness Clearing Statement.

"The definition of insanity is doing the same thing over and over again and expecting different results".
Albert Einstein.

If you've watched Harry Potter, you'll already know that the wand wizards is used to make fire, throw water, make things fly, etc. Well, this Access tool isn't a wand, but it works just the same. It's not magic, but it seems like it. It can't change everything—no, wait, it can, because you're changing your brain every time you use it.

A study published in the Journal of Neuroscience by Leland L. Fleming and Timothy J. McDermott (12) examined how human development, particularly during adolescence, is influenced by synaptic pruning and how this process contributes to improved cognitive control.

The central approach is based on the premise that synaptic pruning, which eliminates redundant neural connections, increases the efficiency of information transfer in the prefrontal cortex. This improved efficiency is key to more effective communication between impulse and decision-making as the brain matures.

The team used response inhibition tasks to assess dynamic changes in neural activity between early and late adolescence. They observed that in late adolescence, neural activity declines more rapidly, which is associated with faster behavioral responses, a sign of greater efficiency in neuronal communication.

These patterns match computational models that predict that synaptic pruning optimizes brain connectivity by strengthening key connections and eliminating redundant ones.

In more digestible terms,

Your brain stores only what is useful and what it has recorded as a learning experience for two purposes:

1. saving energy.
2. surviving.

If something in your brain is inconsistent, synaptic pruning is responsible for erasing that neuronal pathway to make room for new connections.

I'm going to show you how your brain generates a resource, in a very simple way.

Surely when you were in school, you had many classmates whom you loved very much and whom you addressed by name. Do you remember the names of all your classmates today? If you remember them all today, you're an exception to the rule. If you don't remember them, your brain has performed a synaptic pruning process, because there are no longer any anchors. There's no more school, no more teachers, no more need. Consequently, there's no longer any coherence in remembering those names.

If you still hang out with any of those friends today, you probably know their name, you remember where they live, and if they're very close, you'll even remember their birthday.

As you'll see, not all information is erased; only that which your brain deems no longer useful.

And although it's somewhat imperceptible, every time you think about something or someone, there's a chemical response in your body, which triggers a sensation.

David del Rosario in his book The Book Your Brain Doesn't Want to Read. He christened this phenomenon "PENSACION"[2]. This is a thought that has a sensation anchored to the body.

For example, if you think about fire, you don't feel like you're burning, but you have the cognitive concept (thought) that you can get burned if you get close to it (sensation). This concept serves as a survival resource.

Now comes the anecdote.

I grew up in a Christian home. Throughout my childhood, I received the information that sex is inappropriate, that it's sinful, and that it's dirty. When I reached my teens and my sex hormones began to be produced in my body, between the ages of 13 and 15, biologically, I would start thinking about sex and automatically experience an uncomfortable feeling in my body (let's call it anxiety) that told me, "This is bad, it's a sin."

Time passed, and I increasingly struggled with the feeling of anxiety when I thought about sex. Until the day came when I stopped thinking about it and started living it.

It was such a beautiful thing, but at the same time, it generated so much guilt that I wanted to run away and finish quickly so I could stop feeling guilty.

My brain created a neural pathway around sex, which prevented me from enjoying my sexual encounters. Until I discovered this tool, I started using it every night, and everything began to change.

Let's play a little. Think about sex and be aware of the sensation in your body. Don't think, feel, and be brutally honest with yourself.

---

[2] Translator's note. This is a Spanish merger of two words: Thought and Sensation (Pensamiento y Sensación). Since Del Rosario's the book hasn't yet been translated to English, we have decided to keep the Spanish adaptation of the word.

Breathe and let the sensation show in your body. There's no good or bad sensation; just focus on the sensation and repeat the Access Consciousness Clearing Statement after me, "Everything this is, ***RIGHT AND WRONG, GOOD AND BAD, POD AND POC, ALL 100, SHORTS, BOYS, POVADS, CREATIONS, BASES, AND BEYONDS®.***"

Breathe again, think about sex, notice the sensations showing up in your body, and repeat, "Everything this is, ***RIGHT AND WRONG, GOOD AND BAD, POD AND POC, ALL 100, SHORTS, BOYS, POVADS, CREATIONS, BASES, AND BEYONDS.***"

How are you feeling? Think about sex again, feel your body again, and see if anything has changed. If it has, we've just practiced neural pruning. If it hasn't, repeat it two or three more times.

What did we just do? Your brain is trying to understand, and it's as if it's saying, "Wait a minute, I don't understand anything, this sensation I had registered, what is it? Is it good or bad? I don't understand anything. I'd better start erasing this that doesn't make sense."

For a neural pathway to exist, it needs two components: coherence and a concept.

Coherence is, I use this for *this*. I use a blanket to protect myself from the cold.

For coherence to exist, we need a ***concept***, which is having experienced cold.

In my case, the concept was: Sex is a sin and is wrong, and the coherence was: If I have sex, I'm bad.

Do you have any idea how many sexual health disorders originate here?

Every time you deprogram a concept from your brain, you're also changing its coherence. Continuing with the sex example, your brain begins to recognize it as something totally new: not good, not bad, not for something, it just IS, and from this moment on, you can create a new concept that works for you.

The wonderful thing about this is that, once you get to this point, we're not changing a cognitive concept; we're changing the energy that sustains the concept, which is the sensation.

And I know you're going to ask, "What is this and what do all these words mean?"

The interesting thing is that you don't need to understand it for it to work, just use it. But if you really want to know what each word means, you can scan the code to watch the explanatory video or search "Access Consciousness Clearing Statement" in your browser.

Please don't believe me. Use this magical tool, but remember one thing.

Continuing with the Harry Potter analogy. When they first arrived at Hogwarts and didn't have the practice or skill with wands, they had to repeat, repeat, and repeat the spell until it finally worked.

For a neural pathway to exist in your brain, you must have used it hundreds of times, to the point where it has become something automatic. So please don't pretend that with one pass of the clearing statement everything will change. Use it, use it, and use it as many times as necessary, until the sensation disappears from your body.

Until the spell works.

3.8 Create an imprint.

All of life comes to me with ease, joy and glory.®

Use your brain or it will use you.
Juanjo Suárez

Our brain is a wonderful organ, which, as I've already told you, comes with information stored for thousands of years. All the structures and functions I've mentioned are designed to seek out and recognize danger. This isn't wrong, because it's information that has been transmitted ontogenetically since the Stone Age, from generation to generation.

A time when we had to hunt to eat, when you hunted or were hunted, when we had to fight for territory, and you know what? It worked perfectly. And how do I know this? Because we're here today.

All these programs are a series of resources that have helped us survive and preserve our existence.

Now the question is: Do we still live in that environment? I don't think so. It's not the same environment, but our brain manages to continue using those resources because they were useful for thousands of years, for all our ancestors.

Today, instead of chasing prey, we chase professional success. Instead of being stalked by a lion, we're stalked by unpaid bills.

The stimuli are different; the responses are the same.

Our brain is so habituated to functioning this way that it will always focus on danger and the need to survive.

Let me put it this way.

You have a state-of-the-art computer with an 8-gigabyte processor and 1 terabyte of memory. Its functions are state-of-the-art, but the operating system running on it is Windows 92. Doesn't that seem like a waste?

Your machine has enormous capacity, and you can't use that capacity because the operating system is obsolete.

The same thing happens with your brain: the operating system running inside is obsolete. You have an impressive machine, and you're not utilizing its full potential.

How do we change it? By generating a new imprint, a mark that will endure over time.

The Access mantra ***All of life comes to me, with ease, joy, and glory.*** It's the imprint you can engrave on your brain; it's the update to the operating system.

It's giving yourself the ability to move from a state of fight and flight, in which you survive, to a state of expansion, of receiving, of having everything come to you, from a place of ease, joy, and glory.

To create an imprint, you must be stubborn and repeat it so many times that your brain eventually gives up and says, "Okay, I get it."

During World War I, the French doctor Emile Coué(13) promoted the method of conscious autosuggestion. And while there is no formal study with an experimental design published, descriptions of his clinical practice and cases, including hospitalized patients and soldiers wounded during the war, have served as the basis for scientific research today.

What was Coué's approach?

Conscious autosuggestion consists of deliberately repeating, in the present tense and in a calm state, an affirmative phrase to induce changes in mood, body, and health.

The exercise was carried out as follows:

The person would sit in a quiet place to relax, and for 10–20 minutes, a positive phrase would be repeated in the present tense: "Every day, in every way, I am better, better, and better" (this is the most well-known version of the phrases Coué used) or similar phrases focused on improvement and well-being.

The instructions were to formulate the affirmations in the present tense, in terms of already visible progress, and, if possible, accompanied by mental images of healing and a sense of calm. It was to be practiced several times a day, every day.

What kind of results were reported?

The reports from Coué and his followers were largely clinical and anecdotal: they described improvements in people with various problems, including soldiers with neuroses, insomnia, pain, etc.

As I write these pages, I've just taken the May 2025 Global Foundation. In this class, Gary and Dain reemphasized the importance of using this tool, ***"All of life comes to me with ease, joy, and glory."*** Since I've been using it every day, all the time, I can tell you that calm and relaxation are part of my day.

You don't need to be in a meditative state to do this; you can do it while driving, taking a shower, or waiting in line at the bank. You can do it for yourself, in your mind, or out loud: ***"All of life comes to me with ease, joy, and glory."***

When you're faced with a situation that feels like it's holding you back, take a deep breath, use the tools above to regulate the sensations in your body, finish with synaptic pruning, and then find a moment for ***"All of life comes to me with ease, joy, and glory."*** to bring you back to peace and tranquility. It's worth noting that when we say, "Everything Comes," we're not excluding the ugly, the bad, or the complicated.

It's not a tool for falling into absurd positivism; we're programming our brains so that when anything unpleasant comes into our lives, it also comes with total ease.

There are things we can't control, but if we look at them from a different perspective, they'll always bring us greater awareness.

Again, please don't take my word for it. Use the tools, all the ones I shared with you, and see what happens. Conduct your own experiment and draw your own conclusions.

4
One touch, changes everything.

4.1 Access Bars®.

A bridge between mind and body.

"Life is a movement, from infinitely large to infinitely small, everything in this universe is mobile".
Jean Pierre Barral.

First, let's continue with my story. I already mentioned the Access Bars session I took following Bruno's suggestion, and that the most wonderful thing I received from that session was the silence in my head.

In 2024, Dr. Dain taught the BBCOAT class (The Biggest Bars Class of All Time) in Mexico. During those days, he had several interviews, one of which was with Marco Antonio Rengil. In this interview, Dain talked about the Bars and told Marco Antonio: "It's something very simple, very effective, and it works, but I don't know how it works." (If you want to see the interview, scan the code.)

I watched the interview, and more questions arose. And every time you ask a question, you open to a new possibility.

What would result from combining the effectiveness of the Bars with the specificity of Osteopathy? Bingo! Things started to connect.

I'm not going to fill you with anatomical or physiological knowledge; don't be scared, and don't throw the book away.

What I'm going to do is explain to you, in a very simple way, some basic concepts of osteopathy, which apply and fit perfectly with what a Bars session is, anatomically speaking.

One of the things that has characterized me in this life is being stubborn when something gets into my head. I try to be in the eye of the storm, so I dedicated time to reading and rereading the osteopathic concepts that relate to Bars and the reasons for their effectiveness.

Let me tell you upfront, there are things that have no explanation, and I'm okay with that. Energy cannot be measured easily, even more so when its origin is as changeable as a human being.

I'm going to introduce you to James L. Oschman, who conducted a study in 2000 called "Cell Modification by Electromagnetic Fields. The Journal of Alternative and Complementary Medicine." (14)

In his work, he was able to demonstrate that cells in the human body have the ability to change in response to chemical, mechanical, and electromagnetic stimuli.

His approach is more closely related to bioenergetics, cellular communication, and the influence of energy fields on cells. This study opened the possibility of explaining what happens in our hands when we touch a body.

In one part of their study, they were able to demonstrate that a sustained touch (mechanical stimulus) generates changes at the level of the cell membrane and the intracellular matrix, where DNA is located.

This membrane responds to stimuli such as heat and pressure, which causes the membrane density to change and the stimulus to penetrate the matrix.

Now I wonder: Is it possible that with a touch we can modify the structure of cellular memory? Run your Bars and investigate it yourself.

This is one of the principles we use in osteopathy: connecting with the tissue until you feel the change and modification within it. A simple example: When you put butter in your hand, the semi-solid structure of the butter, upon contact with your hand and the heat that your body naturally emanates, generates a change in surface tension (this causes the butter to change shape) and in the cell membrane (this causes the butter to change state from solid to liquid), and our eyes see the butter begin to melt.

And if we add to this another aspect, that our bodies are electrical and that our cells have an electromagnetic charge, we are not only exerting a mechanical stimulus (pressure) or a physical stimulus (heat), but also an electromagnetic stimulus.

Microscopically, I have no proof; Oschman was able to observe that this is possible. I have been able to observe it in large tissues.

There is another study conducted by Michael Meaney and Moshe Szyf (15), which showed that changes in the mood of people with chronic stress can be generated through physical contact. The people who participated in the study expressed that after the sessions, they felt more accepted and more connected to themselves.

In February 2024, I had the opportunity to take my first 3-day Body Class with Dr. Glenna Rice. I attended this class with many questions and concerns.

Knowing that Glenna is also a physical therapist, it was an opportunity to question our training.

For me, it seemed illogical that you touch the body without an anatomical reference and expect a change, so one of my questions was:

"You are also a physiotherapist, you know about the body, its structure and function, you know that it works under parameters that govern matter, how is it possible that as soon as you lay your hands on someone, the body begins to change?"

Without knowing it, I was opening Pandora's box to countless answers and research that I've shared with you here.

Glenna, in her enormous kindness, responded: "You're right. The body, as matter, requires a series of steps for change. If I touch here, it responds there, and it's a process that, to a certain extent, requires stimulus and time.

But if we go further, the body is made up of systems: systems by organs, organs by cells, and cells by atoms. In short, we are energy. To work with energy, all that's required is to be that space of energy."

A simple, but effective answer. Matter is sustained by energy, something Dain always says: "Science has proven that 99.99% of a wall is energy." Well, you're not a wall, but that applies to you too.

Why am I telling you this? Because Access tools are energetic; they're designed for that, to transform energy. The Access Consciousness Clearing Statement, the verbal tools, Access Bars, the Access Body Processes, they all change energy and invite us to increasingly become that space where we are only energy.

But if this concept isn't enough for you, I want you to know that your brain changes, your structure changes, and the body changes too. Your touch is something wonderful that also influences matter, on the physical world, on the body.

Now let me talk to you about anatomy.

Our brain is connected to a wiring system called the nervous system. Its length is approximately 100,000 kilometers. With your nervous system, you can circle the planet Earth, not once, but twice. And you're thinking you're so little.

Some of those nerves are in your skull and face, and they look something like this. Those yellow lines are your nerves.

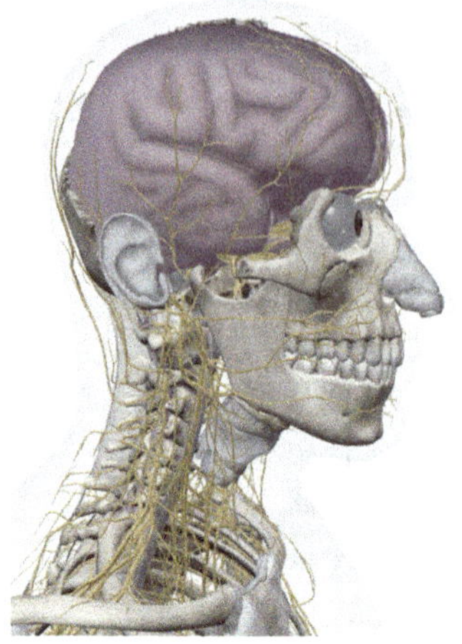

Fuente: Visible Body

They run from deep to superficial, that is, from inside the brain to the outside (many of them are located between the skull and the epidermis).

Among their many functions are facial movements, sensitivity, and conveying information from the sense organs to the brain. They encode visual, auditory, olfactory, gustatory, and tactile stimuli and transform them into nerve impulses (electrical). These nerve impulses reach your brain, and it immediately produces a response.

If you've already taken a Bars class, you've probably noticed that we place our fingers on some of the structures I detailed in the previous chapter. And if you haven't yet, I hope this information is the impulse you were looking for.

A pathway of the *optic nerve* passes beneath our fingers when we touch the *joy and sadness* points. This mechanical, physical, and electromagnetic stimulus influences the information we see.

Beneath our fingers in *the implant band* is the Fusiform Gyrus of the Temporal Lobe, which is the structure responsible for humanizing concepts. In other words, it's the area that tells you: "If you make money differently than your dad would, you're disrespecting him. If you have a different relationship than your mom had, you're disrespecting her." And so on, it associates everyday things with the faces of familiar people. Is it a coincidence that the implant band is here? I don't think so.

Because in fact, the implanted concepts come from the people we assign the status of caregivers in our early childhood: "This person knows more than I do," "This person takes care of me, guides me."

This structure in your brain is responsible for sustaining all these points of view, associated with people.

I have thought of something that might help. You'll be able to recognize that feeling embarrassed isn't the same as remembering the time a family member told you, "Don't embarrass me." Feeling guilty isn't the same as feeling guilty for having let someone down. Perhaps one option might be to clean the Distracting Implants while activating the Implant Band.

In addition to *the Fusiform Gyrus of the Temporal Lobe*, also right in the zone of the Implant Band, we find a nerve that is responsible for regulating the body's vital functions and oversees the activating and deactivating the fight-or-flight states. This is the *Vagus Nerve.*

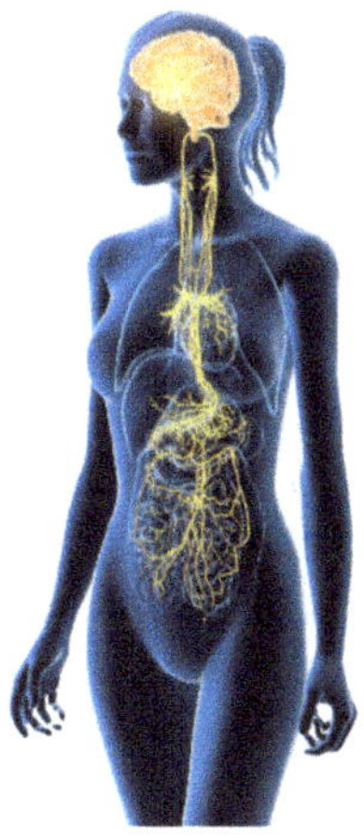

Fuente: Internet

Its function is of vital importance to our body. So much so that its influence on the organic and physiological response to fight-flight-freeze states and its relationship to decision-making has begun to be studied. This nerve divides into two branches: the ventral vagus (relaxes and regulates) and the dorsal vagus (activates and responds). The mere act of placing our hands on this nerve in a subtle and sustained manner will influence tension, viscoelasticity, and the transmission of information, similar to what happens with butter.

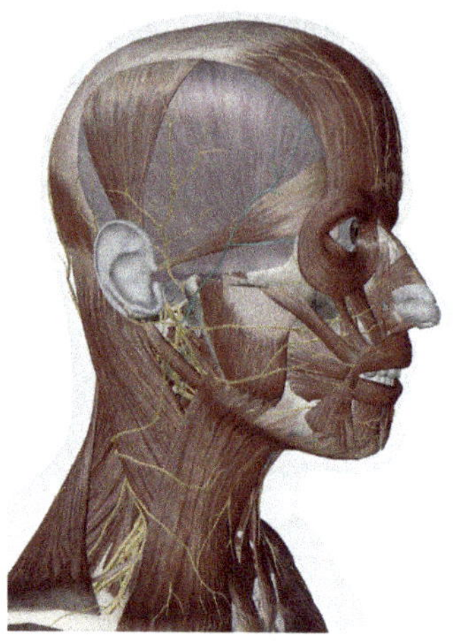

Fuente: Visible Body

Every time you subtly place your hands on this area, you can be present with changes in the person's autonomic system: changes in breathing from shallow to deep, prolonged exhalations (sighs), saccadic eye movements (side to side eye movements), peristaltic sounds (sounds in the stomach), and a decrease in the temperature of the upper and lower limbs. These are signs that the person is entering vagotonia (a state of tissue repair). This is why a Bars session, in addition to creating this space on an energetic level, also invites our body to receive, because it moves out of the fight-or-flight state. In this state, your brain is programmed to attack, defend, and react.

It's worth noting that this vagus nerve also runs through the face and is located right on the Healing, Forms and Structures, Time, Space, and Communication Bars.

It makes perfect biological and physiological sense that the Bars bring about this change in the way we perceive time, our body's functions, and communication, because we are stimulating a nerve that controls people's reactivity.

The aging toaster is located along the path of the Greater Occipital Nerve or Arnold's Nerve, which is responsible for giving sensitivity and tone to the skin of the skull and face.

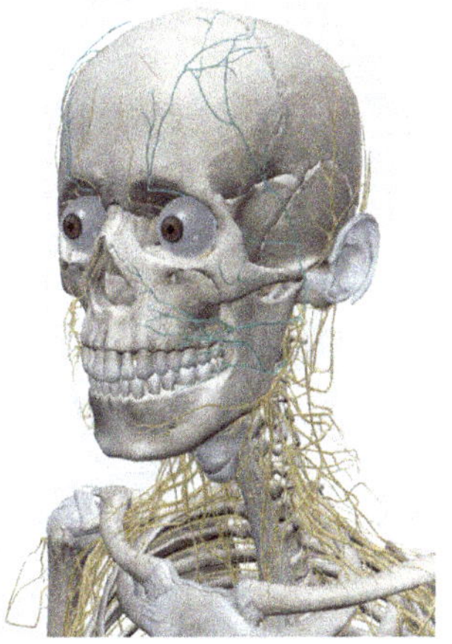

Fuente: Visible Body

Part of *the greater auricular nerve* is under our fingers on the *kindness, gratitude, peace, and calm* Bar, modifying what we hear.

The *trigeminal nerve* is responsible for innervating the meninges, which is a system that protects, nourishes, and cleanses our brain. This nerve runs through much of our skull, as seen in the following image.

When we place our hands on this nerve, we are giving our brain a "massage," thus improving its nutrition. This translates into a state of relaxation and mental clarity. It is one of the most important nerves in communication, as it is responsible for recognizing and interpreting facial gestures.

By exploring these anatomical structures, we can recognize the impact of the bars and why this gentle touch changes many of the concepts we hold in our minds.

I don't mean to say this is true, but it is a concept we use in osteopathy: understanding anatomy, providing appropriate and specific stimulation to the body, and waiting for the body to do what it knows how to do. To regulate itself. This information could help you reach more people, who focus more on the physical.

There are two types of people in the world: those to whom you say, "Come try it," and they jump into the void; others who require a more logical, tangible, and scientific explanation. For this second group, perhaps this makes a little sense. What else is possible with this information?

Let's get off the head and brain and into the body.

Your body is a conglomeration of billions of cells that are constantly changing. There are between 30 and 37 billion cells in your body, which communicate with each other and perform specific functions. When you think of your body as a rigid structure, you buy into the point of view that your only destiny is deterioration.

We were always told that the human body was a kind of "machine with fixed parts": we were born with a certain number of cells, "especially in the brain," and as we grew older, we just lost them. However, the research of Jonas Frisén at the Karolinska Institutet radically changed this view. [16]

Frisén and his team developed an ingenious method: they took advantage of the trace of carbon-14 left in the atmosphere after nuclear tests in the mid-20th century. This radioactive imprint acts as a marker in the DNA of cells, allowing them to calculate their age and, thus, estimate how often they are renewed in different tissues.

The results were revealing:

The skin and intestines show an accelerated rate of regeneration, with constant cell turnover within days or weeks.

The liver renews itself slowly but continuously.

The heart, previously considered incapable of regeneration, has shown that its cells also renew themselves, albeit at a much slower rate (around 1% per year in young adults).

And perhaps most surprising: the brain, specifically the hippocampus, maintains the capacity to produce new neurons throughout life.

This finding reminds us that the body is not static, but an organism in perpetual transformation, a constant dance between destruction and creation. From the perspective of neuroscience and from tools like Access Consciousness, understanding that we are designed to renew ourselves opens the possibility of trusting that change is not only possible, but natural.

Once again, if science has managed to demonstrate that our bodies are constantly regenerating, then why do we age? ***Your point of view creates your reality.***

Bruce Lipton is a renowned cell biologist and science communicator who has popularized concepts related to epigenetics and the influence of the environment on genetic expression and cellular regeneration. His work focuses on how cells are influenced not only by their DNA, but also by external factors, such as environmental conditions, thoughts, emotions, and beliefs.

His line of research seeks to show the cell as an manipulable system: Lipton maintains that cells are not predestined by their DNA, but rather, their behavior and function can be modified by environmental signals.

When Bruce Lipton was working as a cell biologist at the University of Wisconsin, he performed a simple but profoundly revealing experiment. He grew embryonic stem cells in Petri dishes and divided them into several groups.

All the cells were initially genetically identical.

The difference lay in the culture medium, the "biological soil" that nourished the cells.

In one dish, the medium was enriched to promote the formation of bone tissue.

In another, the medium encouraged the generation of muscle tissue.

In a third, the medium stimulated the development of fat cells.

The result was surprising: different types of tissue emerged from the same stem cells, depending solely on the environment in which they grew.

What did this experiment demonstrate?

Fuente: Architecture of human living fascia. Gimberteau

This finding led Lipton to a key conclusion:

Cell destiny is not dictated solely by genes but is strongly influenced by the environment.

What happens in the "external environment" is transformed into chemical signals that activate or silence certain genes within the cell.

Lipton proposes that our beliefs and perceptions function as that environment: they are the "internal environment" that influences the biology of our cells. He explains all of this in detail in his book The Biology of Belief. [(17)]

Just think about it: when you cut your skin, a scab forms, followed by new skin; if you hit a nail and it falls off, after a while your body regenerates a new nail; if you bite your tongue, after a few days, your body has repaired your tongue, and it never makes mistakes; it knows which tissue needs to regenerate in each part of the body.

Ask yourself, if these tissues have the ability to repair and regenerate, why don't the others? Couldn't that be just an interesting point of view?

In osteopathy, there are also physical properties that have been measured in the body, these are viscoelasticity and tensegrity.

Viscoelasticity. It is the property of tissues to recover their elasticity and viscosity when subjected to constant thermal (heat) and mechanical (stretching) stimulation. If the stimulus exceeds the time barrier, it is enough to generate a change in the surface tension of the cell membrane. This means that when you are running Access Bars and place your hands on a particular Bar, you are not only changing the information that travels through that nerve, but you are also restoring its ability to stretch and move.

In other words, you are lubricating the nervous system, which translates into greater flexibility in the person's body. But why in the entire body, if you are only touching the head? This is where this other property comes in.

Tensegrity. To talk about tensegrity, we must talk about Richard Buckminster Fuller [(17)] (1895-1983), who introduced the term Tensegrity. It's a topic I love, and I could make a whole chapter out of it, but that's not the point.

Richard was able to demonstrate that if a structure is interconnected, the stress exerted at one point is distributed and transferred to the entire structure. His model is used today for the construction of bridges and earthquake-resistant structures, and it's also found in your body.

The person who investigated this phenomenon in the human body is Jean-Claude Guimberteau, co-founder and scientific director of the Institut Aquitain de la Main. He discovered a structure that revolutionized the way we view the body and its movement. This structure is fascial tissue, or Fascia [(18)].

Fascia is the tissue that connects the entire body—when I say everything, I mean everything. It's given a name based on the tissue it covers, for example: Peri-toneum (fascia that covers the visceral organs), peri-neurium (fascia that covers the nerves), peri-osteum (fascia that covers the bones), and so on. But it's always the same. This membrane covers absolutely everything in the body and also has the ability to transmit chemical and mechanical information.

If a person has tension in their head, face, or neck, when you relax that area with your touch, you are influencing their entire body, all its structures. Access Bars aren't just about feeling good or freeing your mind; Bars have the ability to change your entire body if you're willing to acknowledge and embrace it.

A recent article from the Clinical Yoga Institute, titled: The Impact of Fascia on Emotional Trauma: Unveiling the Connection, published in 2024, [20], was able to demonstrate that fascia is not only a physical support structure, but a tissue that preserves emotional memories and trauma. This connection is receiving increasing scientific support today.

Fascia can retain traumatic experiences, as it can be clinically observed. Releasing fascial tension simultaneously releases repressed emotions, or what can be called cellular memory.

Fascia is highly sensitive and connected to the autonomic nervous system. When it is tense or restricted by trauma, it interferes with emotional regulation and maintains the body in a prolonged state of stress.

Visceral fascial tightness can manifest as chronic pain, muscle tension, or physical discomfort, reflecting trauma that the body has been unable to process.

This study confirms something we discuss in Bars classes: the release of thoughts, feelings, emotions, and traumas, without the need to make this a cognitive or re-traumatizing process for the person.

Remember your point of view creates your reality. What reality would you like to create every time you give or receive a Bars session or an Access Body Process™?

4.2 Some science on Bars.

Studies and research that have been carried out.

"Experience is the mother of science"
Immanuel Kant.

It's difficult to put into physical terms what happens when you facilitate an Access Bars class or receive a Bars session, especially because each person is unique; their thoughts and inner perception generate variability that is difficult to quantify. Despite this, in 2001, Dr. Terry Hope conducted a study to understand the effects of Access Bars on people diagnosed with depression and anxiety. The result was a significant change in brain waves, which shifted from beta to alpha, which is reflected in people's behavior as states of calm, tranquility, and cerebral coherence. Symptoms associated with anxiety and depression also decreased considerably. These changes were obtained after a one-hour session and are the same changes that would be achieved after practicing six hours of meditation. If you'd like to learn more about this research, you can scan the code to see the explanation provided by neuroscientist Dr. Jeffrey L. Fannin.

During the last Access Global Foundation class in Prague, in May 2025, a new study was also conducted in which subjects' vital signs were taken before and after an Access Bars session, blood samples were taken to observe changes in blood chemistry, and biofeedback measurements were performed to measure the level of brain-heart coherence. To see more about this study, you can scan this code.

Similarly, in November 2024, in Cuenca, Ecuador, we gathered a group of Access Bars facilitators and practitioners to conduct an experimental study on the influence of Access Bars on blood cortisol levels, stress perception, and sleep quality in people diagnosed with fibromyalgia.

To do this, we asked the question: Can Access Bars be an alternative to drug treatment for people with fibromyalgia? We were able to verify after the study was conducted that it could. Below I present a summary of the case analysis, the methodology used, and the results.

Methods: Post hoc case series (hypothesis-generating). Seven adults diagnosed with fibromyalgia, without medications known to interfere with cortisol levels, were included. Two fasting cortisol draws on Day 1 (7:00) and Day 2 (7:00), with an 80-minute Access Consciousness Bars session in between. Stress: PSS-14. Sleep: PSQI global.

Indicators:

1. Objective biomarker: serum cortisol (μg/dL), measured before and after the session.
2. Perceived Stress Scale (PSS-14): scores range from 0 to 50, with higher values indicating greater stress. Data were collected before and after the first and second blood draws.
3. Global PSQI Sleep Quality: average hours of sleep per night. / Difficulty falling asleep: qualitative scale (mild difficulty / no difficulty).

Results: Serum Cortisol

Mean reduction of 2.73 μg/dL (–20.5%), with negative differences in all cases. Bootstrap 95% confidence interval of the mean difference: [–3.68, –1.86].

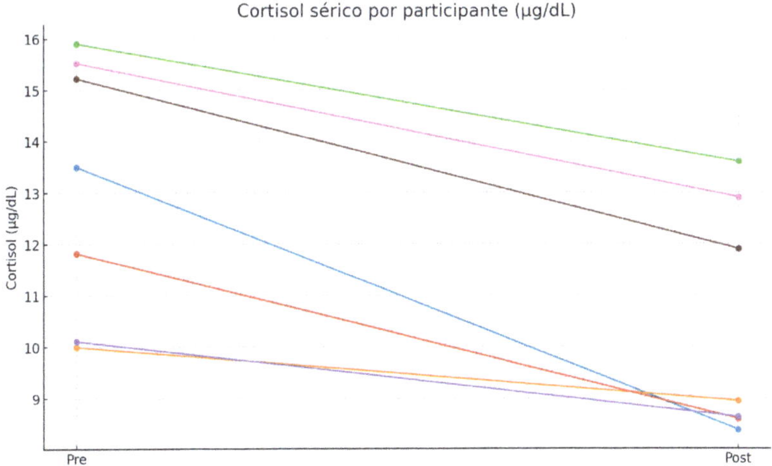

Each color represents a subject; the image shows the reduction in cortisol levels before and after the session.

Results: Perceived Stress Scale

- Pre-session mean: 31.4 (SD = 7.07)
- Post-session mean: 22.1 (SD = 4.95)
- Mean difference: −9.3 points (SD = 8.73)
- Median difference: −8 points
- Average percentage reduction: 27.0%

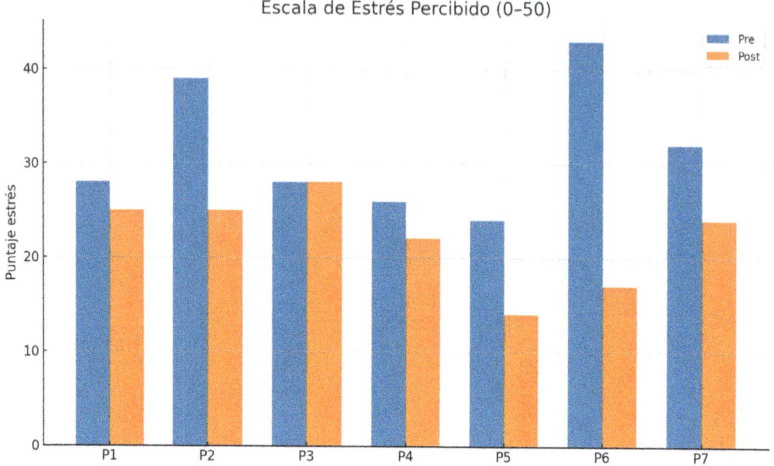

A clear reduction in the stress score was observed, with most participants showing significant decreases.

Results: Sleep

Sleep Hours:

- Before the session: Range 4–6 hours (average ≈ 5 h).
- After the session: Range 6–8 hours (average ≈ 7 h).
- Average increase: +2 hours per participant.

Difficulty falling asleep:

- Improved: 4 participants (57.1%)
- No change (had no difficulty before): 3 participants (42.9%)
- Worsened: 0

More than half of the participants experienced a clear improvement in ease of falling asleep.

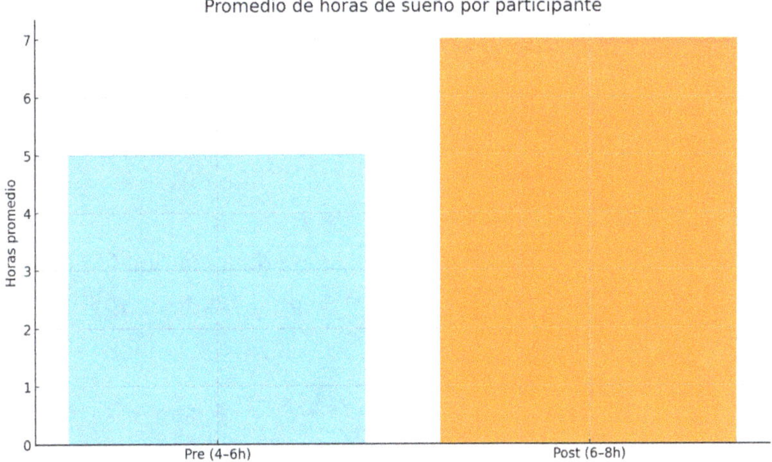

In addition to these research results, we also had to exclude a subject from the study whose laboratory tests showed that his body does not produce cortisol, a hormone that acts as a master regulator of the body's balance, allowing it to adapt to internal and external changes. In excess (due to chronic stress) it can cause harm: immunosuppression, abdominal weight gain, anxiety, or insomnia. Deficiency causes fatigue, weakness, and low blood pressure. What's interesting about this case is that the person is a high-performance athlete, his activity level is intense, and his body's recovery capacity is stable. I mention this to further question normality in health.

What is normal? What happens when a person (unknowingly) is pushing the limits of what is established as normal? What are we and our bodies capable of that we haven't yet recognized?

While financial resources were a limitation in the research, this effort is a seed that will bear fruit in the future, with research in which we can obtain statistically significant results. In addition to being a seed, it also represents an alternative treatment for people with this diagnosis.

At this point, I would like to thank Dr. Geovanny Sanchez, who was responsible for data analysis and interpretation. He is the person who made it possible to put into figures what we knew was there.

To Dr. Sonia Cabrera and her clinical laboratory, who were responsible for taking blood samples before and after the Bars session.

To Emilia Reyes, who was involved in the logistics and setting up the space for the study.

I am infinitely grateful to this group of facilitators and practitioners for accepting the call, for putting their hands into this study, for their dedication to always strive for more.

And of course, to the volunteers who gave their consent to be study subjects, for lending their minds, their bodies, and their willingness. I have infinite gratitude.

5
Conclusion.

5.1 Awaken your potential

It was always you.

> "*You are not a human being in search for a spiritual experience. You are a spiritual being immersed in a human experience. Inside you lies the same force that creates worlds*"
>
> *Wayne Dyer.*

In the last few years that I've been able to share and take classes with several facilitators, they've all invited me to go to a different place. And that's where I would like to invite you too. To recognize that You and I are the source of everything. That there is nothing outside of you, that you are the creator of the reality you are seeing.

This book is a reaffirmation of this idea. Your body and brain are equipped with everything you require to choose a greater life. If you know where to direct your focus, your energy, and your choices.

As I've shown you, the Access tools are wonderful and using them allows us to continually update our operating system. They allow us to break out of the limited reality we implanted for ourselves with our unconscious choices.

Now that you know what you chose in the past and what you were creating with your brain, regain your focus and choose differently.

If something doesn't expand you, choose differently; if something doesn't change, dig deep inside yourself, use your structures, and use the tools to make that journey, and then get your Bars run.

This book isn't about telling you how to do things; it's a reminder that you know what's best for you. That if you access your knowing and abilities, you can change your reality, transforming everything from within, from your neural connections, from your brain structures.

I'm passionate about human beings, about how they work. I've always tried and continue to try to understand behavior, patterns, and motivations.

Along this path, I've been able to learn and deepen my knowledge of the Enneagram, Psychoneuroimmunology, Transgenerational Psychology, and Biological Sense. Each tool has allowed me to add a little more to this journey of understanding.

Now, there's a big difference between understanding and changing. For a long time, I understood where I was working from, but change didn't happen until Access found me or I found it.

With these tools, change came. Because it doesn't require understanding something to be changed; it requires you, your constant choice. It's just recognizing that something doesn't expand you, that something doesn't work for you, and choosing differently, not because it's wrong, but simply because there's a different possibility.

Your brain is yours, and the only one who can use it to create something greater is you. No one is going to choose for you. In fact, when we were children, many of our choices were made by others, and if you're reading these pages today, it's because you questioned those choices and know there's something new for you.

A Bars session can be the beginning of something wonderful, as it was for Dain, who was on the verge of ending his life (If you want to know more about his story, you can read his book, Being You, Changing the World). As it was for Rafael (the facilitator with whom I did my first Foundation Class), who was diagnosed with chemical depression, something doctors said was incurable; as it was for me, to stop hearing so many voices in my head that only paralyzed me because I didn't know which one to listen to.

Some time ago I said no to teaching at the Osteopathy Institute and the University, today I find myself facilitating Bars classes, body processes and Access introductory classes because it is what expands me, I went against many people and "disappointed" many others, but you know what, I have not disappointed myself.

If you could never fail, what would you choose?

If there was no one to disappoint, what would you choose?

If you could change your reality, choice after choice, would you do it?

There's a question I've left for last, which is one of Access's wonderful tools, which I use all the time: ***What energy am I being?***

It's an invitation to look at yourself for a moment. When you are "being," your brain is producing a series of chemicals and neurotransmitters that send signals to your body and vice versa. These signals are associated with what you perceive with your sense organs and are linked to the information that enters your brain through thoughts and mental images.

If you look at a sunset, it can be a beautiful sight, but if you hold the idea in your head that you are alone and feel incomplete in that wonderful moment, every time you look at a sunset, your brain will produce the chemicals you've just associated with the sunset, and you'll begin to experience loneliness, sadness, or lack. The same thing happens with money, with people, with work, and with many other anchors.

Ask yourself every moment of the day, ***"What energy am I being?"*** And give yourself permission to choose something different. If you're making debt more valuable and relevant and you're being lack, change your energy. Remember, you don't need to understand to change.

If you realize, Access tools are a game; they're an invitation to constantly question yourself, like when you were a child: Why? What is this for? What if I don't want to? Do it again, recover your questioning until you find coherence between what you're thinking and what you're feeling in your body. When you achieve this, you will be developing the ability to live in total presence.

Love your brain, because it has brought you here, alive. Don't judge it; recognize its infinite potential. And now, go ahead and play with it, develop all that potential you have, install the updates, and use the Access tools so you can get the most out of your computer.

Please, always follow your knowledge, always use the tools with awareness of what will create more.

Dear Human Being. Welcome to your new life.

Disclaimer

All the Access tools described in this book were developed by Gary Douglas and Dain Heer and are the property of Access Consciousness®. Tools such as the mantra and the clearing statement are the intellectual property of Access Consciousness. If you'd like to learn more about Access Consciousness, you can visit the website www.accessconsciousness.com Here you'll find all the information on the types of bars and different topics, such as business, money, entities, relationships, and more.

Bibliographic References.

1. MacLean, P. D. (1960).Scientistne brain in evolution: A new view of brain function. American Scientist, 48(2), 169-179.
2. Soon, C. S., Brass, M., Heinze, H.-J., & Haynes, J.-D. (2008). Unconscious determinants of free decisions in the human brain. Nature Neuroscience, 11(9), 543–545. https://doi.org/10.1038/nn.2132
3. Joëls, M., Baram, T. Z., & Sapolsky, R. M. (2010). Stress and the brain: individual variability and the inverted-U. Nature Neuroscience, 13(11), 1334–1340. https://doi.org/10.1038/nn.2628 The journal, volume, issue, and pages correspond to the correct data from the article published in 2010.
4. Grinberg-Zylberbaum, J., & Ramos, J. (1993). Human communication and the electrophysiological activity of the brain. Physics Essays, 6(2), 292–302. https://doi.org/10.4006/1.3029160
5. Rizzolatti, G., Fogassi, L., & Luppino, G. (1990). Mirror neurons: premises, explanations, and functions. Neuropsychologia, 28(5), 593–601. https://doi.org/10.1016/0028-3932(90)90007-T
6. Poponin, V. V., & Gariaev, P. P. (1997). The DNA phantom effect. Proceedings of the Russian Academy of Sciences, 351(4), 1079–1082.
7. Simons, D. J., & Chabris, C. F. (1999). Gorillas in our midst: Sustained inattentional blindness. *Perception*, *28*(9), 1059–1074. https://doi.org/10.1068/p281059

8. LeDoux, JE, Iwata, J., Cicchetti, P., & Reis, DJ (1988). Different projections of the central amygdaloid nucleus mediate autonomic and behavioral correlates of conditioned fear. *Journal of Neuroscience*, 8(7), 2517 – 2529.

9. Crum, A. J., Langer, E. J., & Chalmers, D. (2011). The effect of expectation on pain: A randomized clinical trial. *Psychosomatic Medicine*, 73(7), 565-571. https://doi.org/10.1097/PSY.0b013e31822d6e4d

10. Berridge, K. C., & Robinson, T. E. (1998). What is the role of dopamine in reward: Hedonic impact, reward learning, or incentive salience? *Brain Research Reviews*, 28(3), 309-369. https://doi.org/10.1016/S0165-0173(98)00019-2

11. Cumming, J., & Williams, S. E. (2012). The role of imagery in enhancing the performance of athletes. *The Sport Psychologist*, 26(2), 203-222. https://doi.org/10.1123/tsp.26.2.203

12. Fleming, L. L., & McDermott, T. J. (2024). Cognitive control and neural activity during human development: Evidence for synaptic pruning. Journal of Neuroscience, 44(26), e0373242024. https://doi.org/10.1523/JNEUROSCI.0373-24.2024

13. Coué, É. (1922). La maîtrise de soi par l'autosuggestion. Paris: Félix Alcan.

14. Oschman, J. L. (2000). Cell communication with electromagnetic fields. *The Journal of Alternative and Complementary Medicine*, 6(5), 491-503. https://doi.org/10.1089/10755530050195359

15. Meaney, M. J., & Szyf, M. (2005). Environmental programming of stress responses through DNA methylation: Life at the interface between a dynamic environment and a fixed genome. *Dialogues in Clinical Neuroscience*, 7(2), 103–123.

16. Spalding, K. L., Bergmann, O., Alkass, K., Bernard, S., Salehpour, M., Huttner, H. B, & Frisén, J. (2013). Dynamics of hippocampal

neurogenesis in adult humans. Cell, 153(6), 1219–1227. https://doi.org/10.1016/j.cell.2013.05.002

17. Lipton, B. H. (2005). The biology of belief: Unleashing the power of consciousness, matter & miracles. Hay House.

18. Fuller, R. B. (1961). *Tensegrity: The new science of structural principles*. Self-published.

19. Guimberteau, J.-C. (2014). The dynamic fascia. *The Journal of the American Academy of Orthopaedic Surgeons*, 22(3), 161–164.

20. Corena Hammer. (2024, 22 de junio). The impact of fascia on emotional trauma: Unveiling the connection. Clinical Yoga Institute. Recovered from https://www.clinicalyogainstitute.com/post/the-impact-of-fascia-on-emotional-trauma-unveiling-the-connection

About the Author

Juan José Suárez (Juanjo) graduated professionally from the University of Cuenca with a degree in Physiotherapist, then dedicated himself to studying for the joy of learning. He has been continuing his training in Osteopathy with the Barral Institute since 2016. He studied an Expertise in Psychoneuroimmunology at the Tech Institute of Mexico and became certified as an Enneagram Facilitator with the Enneagram Coaching Center of Mexico. He is currently pursuing Bodhi Medicine training. His training has allowed him to shape Biology, Belief, and Energy, the program he uses to support people in their health journeys and in personal situations.

Since 2022, he has integrated Access Consciousness tools into his life and practice. Having observed unusually rapid and lasting changes in both his personal and professional spheres, he has also dedicated himself to facilitating these tools, as a BF, BPF, and CFMW of Access Consciousness.

www.ingramcontent.com/pod-product-compliance
Lightning Source LLC
LaVergne TN
LVHW050541100826
845148LV00002B/643

* 9 7 8 1 6 3 4 9 3 7 6 3 4 *